DECLUTTERING YOUR DIGITAL LIFE

How to Organize Your Digital Space and Boost Productivity

by

Joseph Owens

Table of Contents

BOOK OVERVIEW

In today's digital age, we rely heavily on technology to organize our lives, communicate with others, and complete our work. We use our computers, smartphones, tablets, and other devices to store vast amounts of data, from personal photos and documents to work-related files and emails. However, this convenience also comes with a downside: clutter.

Just as physical clutter can cause stress and reduce productivity, digital clutter can have a similar effect. Having a cluttered digital space can make it difficult to find what you need quickly, and it can also slow down your devices and make them more prone to crashes and errors. In this article, we will explore how to declutter your digital life and organize your digital space to boost productivity.

The first step in decluttering your digital life is to assess the current state of your digital space. Take a look at your computer desktop, your email inbox, your smartphone apps, and your cloud storage accounts. Do you have a lot of files and folders that you rarely use? Are there duplicate files taking up space on your hard drive? Are your apps and software up-to-date? By answering these questions, you can identify the areas that need the most attention.

Once you have identified the areas that need decluttering, it's time to get started. Here are some tips for organizing your digital space and boosting productivity:

- Clean up your desktop: Your computer desktop is often the first thing you see when you turn on your computer, so it's important to keep it organized. Delete any shortcuts or files that you no longer need, and create folders for the remaining items. This will make it easier to find what you need quickly.

- Organize your files and folders: Take the time to organize your files and folders in a way that makes sense to you. For example, you could create folders for different projects or clients, or you could organize your files by type (e.g., photos, documents, music). Make sure to label your folders clearly so that you can find what you need quickly.

- Delete duplicate files: Duplicate files can take up a lot of space on your hard drive and make it difficult to find the original file when you need it. Use a duplicate file finder to locate and delete any duplicate files on your computer.

- Archive old files: If you have files that you no longer need but don't want to delete, consider archiving them. You can move them to an external hard drive or cloud storage account to free up space on your computer.

- Keep your email inbox organized: Your email inbox can quickly become overwhelmed with messages, making it difficult to find the messages that matter. Create folders for different types of messages (e.g., work, personal, newsletters), and use filters to automatically sort incoming messages into the appropriate folder.

- Unsubscribe from unwanted newsletters: If you receive a lot of newsletters that you no longer read, unsubscribe from them. This will reduce the number of emails in your inbox and help you stay focused on the messages that matter.

- Update your software and apps: Keeping your software and apps up-to-date can improve their performance and reduce the risk of security vulnerabilities. Set your devices to automatically update when new versions become available.

- Backup your data: It's important to regularly backup your data to prevent the loss of important files. You can use an external hard drive or cloud storage account to backup your files.

By doing these, you can declutter your digital life and boost productivity. You'll be able to find what you need quickly, and your devices will run more smoothly. You may even find that you have more time to focus on the things that matter to you. It's important to note that decluttering your digital life is an ongoing process, and it's something that you will need to revisit regularly. As you continue to use your devices and store new data, you may need to reorganize your files and folders or delete files that are no longer needed.

In addition to the practical benefits of decluttering your digital life, there are also psychological benefits. A cluttered digital space can cause feelings of overwhelm and anxiety, which can negatively impact your overall well-being. By decluttering your digital life, you can create a sense of calm and order that can help you feel more focused and productive. Another important aspect of staying organized in your digital life is to maintain good digital hygiene. This means regularly updating your passwords, avoiding suspicious emails and links, and being mindful of the data you share online.

Decluttering your digital life is an essential step in maintaining a productive and efficient workflow. By taking the time to organize your digital space and implement strategies to stay organized, you can reduce stress, increase focus, and boost your overall well-being. Whether you're a busy professional or a busy parent, decluttering your digital life can help you stay on top of your game and achieve your goals.

CHAPTER 1

INTRODUCTION TO DIGITAL CLUTTER

Definition of digital clutter

In this net generation, technology has revolutionized the way we communicate, work, and live. The rise of digital technology has resulted in an explosion of information and data available at our fingertips. With the ease of creating digital files, it's easy to accumulate large amounts of digital data over time. However, this can lead to digital clutter, which can have negative effects on our productivity, mental well-being, and overall quality of life.

Digital clutter refers to the accumulation of digital files, emails, notifications, and other digital items that are no longer useful or relevant. It can take many forms, including unorganized files, unread emails, unnecessary apps, and excessive notifications. Digital clutter can be caused by various factors, including the reluctance to delete anything, the constant influx of new information, and the inability to manage the sheer volume of data.

One of the most common examples of digital clutter is a cluttered desktop. Many people save files and folders directly to their desktop for easy access, but over time, this can lead to a cluttered and disorganized workspace. Similarly, email inboxes can quickly become cluttered with unread emails, spam, and other unnecessary messages. The notification center of a phone or computer can also become overwhelming with the constant flow of alerts and updates.

Digital clutter can have a significant impact on productivity. When digital spaces are disorganized, it can be challenging to focus on the task at hand, leading to feelings of overwhelm and anxiety. A cluttered desktop or email inbox can make it difficult to find necessary documents or emails when needed, resulting in wasted time and decreased efficiency. Additionally, constant notifications and alerts can cause stress and distract us from important tasks.

Digital clutter can also have negative effects on mental well-being. A study conducted by the University of California, Irvine found that it takes an average of 23 minutes and 15 seconds to refocus after being distracted by a notification. Constant notifications and alerts can lead to decreased focus, increased stress, and even addiction to technology.

There are several strategies for managing digital clutter. One of the most effective strategies is organization. Creating folders and subfolders for digital files can help keep them organized and easy to find. Using filters to sort emails can help manage email inboxes and reduce clutter. Disabling notifications for non-essential apps can also help minimize distractions.

Regularly deleting unnecessary data can also help keep digital clutter at bay. This can include deleting old files, emails, and apps that are no longer useful or relevant. It's important to regularly review digital files and determine whether they are necessary or not. If a file is no longer needed, it should be deleted to avoid clutter.

Another strategy for managing digital clutter is to establish digital boundaries. This can include limiting the amount of time spent on digital devices, turning off notifications during specific times of the day, and minimizing the number of apps and devices used. By setting boundaries, individuals can reduce the amount of digital clutter in their lives and improve their productivity and mental well-being.

One way to implement digital boundaries is to establish a "digital detox." This can involve taking a break from technology for a certain period, such as a day or a weekend. During this time, individuals can focus on other activities, such as reading, spending time with friends and family, or pursuing hobbies. A digital detox can help individuals reset and refocus their attention on what is truly important in their lives.

Digital clutter can also have a significant impact on businesses. When businesses accumulate large amounts of digital clutter, it can lead to decreased productivity, decreased efficiency, and increased costs. Digital clutter can make it difficult to find necessary files or documents, resulting in wasted time and decreased productivity. Additionally, businesses may need to invest in additional storage or hardware to manage the volume of data.

One example of a business affected by digital clutter is a marketing agency. Marketing agencies often deal with a large amount of digital data, including client files, creative assets, and campaign analytics. If these files are not organized and managed effectively, it can lead to a decrease in productivity and efficiency. For example, if a client file cannot be found quickly, it may delay the start of a project, leading to missed deadlines and decreased client satisfaction.

To combat digital clutter in a business setting, it's important to establish clear guidelines for digital organization and management. This can include establishing a file naming convention, creating a shared drive for digital files, and implementing regular file reviews to delete unnecessary data.

In addition to organization, businesses can also implement software and tools to help manage digital clutter. For example, project management tools like Trello or Asana can help keep tasks and projects organized and on track. Collaboration tools like Slack or Microsoft Teams can help reduce the number of emails and notifications exchanged between team members, leading to increased efficiency and decreased clutter.

Another effective strategy for managing digital clutter in a business setting is to implement a "clean desk policy." This policy requires employees to clean up their digital workspace at the end of each day, deleting unnecessary files and organizing remaining files into folders. This policy can help keep digital clutter at bay and improve productivity and efficiency.

Digital clutter can also have a significant impact on our physical spaces. For example, if digital files are not backed up or stored properly, they may take up valuable physical space on a computer or external hard drive. This can lead to the need for additional storage devices or hardware, which can be costly.

In addition, digital clutter can also lead to increased energy usage. When digital devices are constantly running and storing unnecessary data, they require more energy to function. This can lead to increased electricity usage and higher energy bills.

To combat digital clutter's impact on physical spaces, it's important to establish clear guidelines for digital storage and backup. This can include implementing a regular backup schedule, storing digital files on cloud-based services, and using external hard drives or other storage devices for files that need to be accessed offline.

In conclusion, digital clutter is a growing problem in today's digital age. It can have negative impacts on productivity, mental well-being, physical spaces, and even businesses. However, by implementing effective organization and management strategies, individuals and businesses can combat digital clutter and improve their overall quality of life. By taking regular breaks from technology, setting digital boundaries, and establishing clear guidelines for digital organization and storage, we can take control of our digital lives and reduce the negative impacts of digital clutter.

The negative effects of digital clutter on productivity and mental health

Digital clutter refers to the accumulation of digital data, files, and information that can cause stress and anxiety in individuals, leading to negative effects on productivity and mental health. With the increase in the use of technology in our daily lives, the issue of digital clutter has become more prevalent, affecting people of all ages and professions.

The negative effects of digital clutter can impact an individual's productivity by creating a distraction and causing them to spend time sifting through unnecessary files and data. It can also lead to a lack of focus and increased stress, which can have a significant impact on one's mental health.

One of the most significant negative effects of digital clutter on productivity is the time wasted on sifting through unnecessary information. This can lead to decreased efficiency, missed deadlines, and a reduction in the quality of work produced. For example, when an individual spends an excessive amount of time searching for a file, they may become frustrated and lose momentum on their work, leading to delays in project completion.

Digital clutter can also lead to a lack of focus and increased stress, which can have a significant impact on one's mental health. When an individual's digital space is cluttered, it can be overwhelming, leading to feelings of anxiety and stress. The constant bombardment of information can make it difficult to focus on important tasks, leading to decreased productivity and increased stress levels.

Moreover, digital clutter can impact one's ability to prioritize tasks and make decisions effectively. The sheer volume of digital data and files can lead to decision fatigue, where an individual becomes overwhelmed with the number of choices and decisions they have to make. This can lead to procrastination, decreased motivation, and an inability to complete tasks effectively.

The negative effects of digital clutter on productivity and mental health are not limited to individuals but can also impact businesses. Businesses that deal with large amounts of digital data, such as marketing agencies or technology companies, can be particularly affected. Digital clutter can lead to decreased efficiency, missed deadlines, and decreased client satisfaction, ultimately impacting the bottom line.

To combat the negative effects of digital clutter on productivity and mental health, it's important to establish clear guidelines for digital organization and management. This can include establishing a file naming convention, creating a shared drive for digital files, and implementing regular file reviews to delete unnecessary data.

In addition to organization, individuals can also take steps to reduce digital clutter in their personal lives. For example, setting boundaries around technology use, taking regular breaks from screens, and deleting unnecessary apps and files can help reduce the amount of digital clutter in our lives. By doing so, individuals can improve their mental health and increase their productivity.

Moreover, businesses can also implement software and tools to help manage digital clutter. Project management tools like Trello or Asana can help keep tasks and projects organized and on track. Collaboration tools like Slack or Microsoft Teams can help reduce the number of emails and notifications exchanged between team members, leading to increased efficiency and decreased clutter.

Another effective strategy for managing digital clutter in a business setting is to implement a "clean desk policy." This policy requires employees to clean up their digital workspace at the end of each day, deleting unnecessary files and organizing remaining files into folders. This policy can help keep digital clutter at bay and improve productivity and efficiency.

The negative effects of digital clutter on productivity and mental health can also be combated by establishing a regular practice of digital detox. Taking a break from technology can help reduce stress levels, improve mental clarity, and increase productivity. This can be done by setting aside a designated time each day to disconnect from technology, whether it's taking a walk, reading a book, or engaging in another activity that doesn't involve screens, and implementing software and tools to help manage digital clutter, individuals and businesses can reduce the negative impacts of digital clutter on their productivity and mental health.

One important step in reducing digital clutter is to establish a routine for digital organization and management. This can include developing a file naming convention, creating a shared drive for digital files, and regularly reviewing and deleting unnecessary data. By having a system in place for organizing and managing digital data, individuals can save time and reduce stress when searching for important files.

Another strategy for reducing digital clutter is to establish boundaries around technology use. For example, setting aside designated times each day to check emails or social media can help individuals avoid getting distracted by unnecessary notifications and alerts. This can lead to increased focus and productivity, as well as reduced stress levels.

In addition to establishing boundaries around technology use, taking regular breaks from screens can also help reduce the negative effects of digital clutter on mental health. This can involve activities like taking a walk outside, engaging in a hobby, or simply disconnecting from technology for a set period of time each day. By taking time away from screens, individuals can reduce feelings of anxiety and overwhelm, and improve their overall mental wellbeing.

For businesses, implementing software and tools to help manage digital clutter can also be effective in improving productivity and reducing stress levels. Project management tools like Trello or Asana can help keep tasks and projects organized and on track, while collaboration tools like Slack or Microsoft Teams can help reduce the number of emails and notifications exchanged between team members. By streamlining communication and project management, businesses can reduce the amount of digital clutter in their digital space and improve their overall efficiency.

Implementing a "clean desk policy" can also be an effective strategy for reducing digital clutter in a business setting. This policy requires employees to clean up their digital workspace at the end of each day, deleting unnecessary files and organizing remaining files into folders. This can help keep digital clutter at bay and improve productivity and efficiency, as well as reduce stress levels among employees.

Establishing a regular practice of digital detox can also be an effective way to reduce the negative effects of digital clutter on productivity and mental health. This can involve taking a break from technology for a set period of time each day or week, and engaging in activities that don't involve screens. By disconnecting from technology, individuals can reduce feelings of stress and overwhelm, and improve their overall mental wellbeing.

Digital clutter can, therefore, have significant negative effects on productivity and mental health. However, by establishing clear guidelines for digital organization and management, setting boundaries around technology use, taking regular breaks from screens, implementing software and tools to help manage digital clutter, and practicing digital detox, individuals and businesses can reduce the negative impacts of digital clutter and improve their overall efficiency and wellbeing.

CHAPTER 2

ASSESSING YOUR DIGITAL CLUTTER

Identifying the types of digital clutter you have

In order to effectively manage and reduce digital clutter, it is important to first identify the types of clutter that exist in our digital lives. Digital clutter can take many forms, from excessive emails and files to unused apps and subscriptions. By understanding the types of digital clutter we have, we can develop strategies to organize and manage our digital lives more effectively. In this article, we will explore the different types of digital clutter and provide tips for identifying and managing each one.

Email Clutter: Email is a major source of digital clutter for many individuals. It's easy to let emails pile up in our inboxes, making it difficult to find important messages when we need them. The first step in managing email clutter is to go through our inboxes and delete any unnecessary emails. This can include spam, newsletters, and old messages that no longer serve a purpose. Next, we can organize our remaining emails into folders based on topic or priority, making it easier to find important messages when we need them. We can also set up filters to automatically sort incoming emails into specific folders, further reducing the clutter in our inboxes.

Files Clutter: Digital files can also contribute to clutter in our digital lives. It's common to accumulate a large number of files over time, many of which may no longer be necessary. The first step in managing file clutter is to go through our files and delete any that we no longer need. This can include old documents, photos, and videos. We can also organize our remaining files into folders based on topic or purpose, making it easier to find what we need when we need it. Another option is to use cloud storage services like Dropbox or Google Drive, which can help us manage our files more efficiently and free up space on our devices.

App Clutter: Many of us have a large number of apps on our phones and other devices, many of which we may not even use. This can contribute to digital clutter and slow down our devices. The first step in managing app clutter is to go through our apps and delete any that we no longer use or need. We can also organize our remaining apps into folders based on purpose or category, making it easier to find what we need when we need it. It's also a good idea to periodically review our app subscriptions and cancel any that we no longer use or need.

Social Media Clutter: Social media can also contribute to digital clutter in our lives. We may have accounts on multiple platforms, each with its own notifications and updates. The first step in managing social media clutter is to review our accounts and delete any that we no longer use or need. We can also adjust our notification settings to reduce the number of alerts we receive, and unfollow any accounts that no longer serve a purpose. It's also a good idea to set aside designated times each day to check social media, rather than constantly checking throughout the day.

Digital Calendar Clutter: Digital calendars can be a useful tool for organizing our schedules, but they can also contribute to digital clutter if not managed properly. We may have multiple calendars, each with its own events and reminders. The first step in managing digital calendar clutter is to review our calendars and delete any events or reminders that are no longer relevant. We can also consolidate our calendars into a single, unified calendar, making it easier to manage our schedule. It's also important to set reminders and alerts only for events that are truly important, rather than cluttering our calendars with unnecessary notifications.

Thus, digital clutter can take many forms, from excessive emails and files to unused apps and subscriptions. By identifying the types of digital clutter we have and developing strategies to manage them, we can reduce the negative impacts of digital clutter on our productivity and mental health. Some strategies for managing digital clutter include

Evaluating the impact of each type of digital clutter on your life

Digital clutter can have a significant impact on our lives, affecting everything from our productivity and mental health to our overall sense of well-being. In order to effectively manage digital clutter, it's important to understand the different types of digital clutter and how they can impact our lives.

Email Clutter

Email clutter can take many forms, from unread messages to spam and promotional emails. The constant influx of emails can be overwhelming and distracting, making it difficult to focus on important tasks. Email clutter can also lead to missed deadlines and important messages, which can have serious consequences.

To evaluate the impact of email clutter on your life, ask yourself the following questions:

- How many unread emails do you currently have in your inbox?
- How much time do you spend each day checking and responding to emails?
- How often do you miss important messages or deadlines due to email overload?
- How much time do you spend unsubscribing from unwanted emails?

By answering these questions, you can gain a better understanding of how email clutter is affecting your life and develop strategies for managing it.

Digital Files and Documents Clutter

Digital files and documents clutter can include everything from outdated files to duplicates and irrelevant information. This type of clutter can make it difficult to find important documents when you need them and can also take up valuable storage space on your devices.

To evaluate the impact of digital files and documents clutter on your life, ask yourself the following questions:

- How often do you search for a file or document and can't find it?
- How much time do you spend organizing and deleting files?
- How much storage space is taken up by unnecessary files and documents?

- How often do you accidentally save a file in the wrong place or forget where you saved it?

By evaluating these factors, you can determine how much digital files and documents clutter is affecting your life and develop strategies for managing it.

Social Media Clutter

Social media clutter can include everything from unnecessary notifications to an overwhelming number of friends and followers. This type of clutter can be distracting and time-consuming, making it difficult to focus on important tasks and leading to feelings of anxiety and overwhelm.

To evaluate the impact of social media clutter on your life, ask yourself the following questions:

- How much time do you spend on social media each day?
- How often do you check social media throughout the day?
- How much time do you spend responding to notifications?
- How often do you feel overwhelmed or anxious as a result of social media?

By answering these questions, you can gain a better understanding of how social media clutter is affecting your life and develop strategies for managing it.

App Clutter

App clutter can include everything from unused apps to unnecessary notifications and updates. This type of clutter can be distracting and time-consuming, making it difficult to focus on important tasks and leading to feelings of overwhelm and frustration.

To evaluate the impact of app clutter on your life, ask yourself the following questions:

- How many unused apps do you have on your device?
- How often do you receive notifications from apps that you don't use or need?
- How much time do you spend updating apps?

- How much storage space is taken up by unused apps?

By evaluating these factors, you can determine how much app clutter is affecting your life and develop strategies for managing it.

Calendar Clutter

Calendar clutter can include everything from too many events and appointments to multiple calendars that are not synced. This type of clutter can be overwhelming and can lead to missed appointments and deadlines.

To evaluate the impact of calendar clutter on your life, ask yourself the following questions:

- How many events and appointments do you have on your calendar?

- How often do you forget about or miss appointments and deadlines?

- How much time do you spend managing multiple calendars?

- How much time do you spend trying to figure out which events are most important or urgent?

By answering these questions, you can gain a better understanding of how calendar clutter is affecting your life and develop strategies for managing it.

Digital Communication Clutter

Digital communication clutter can include everything from unread messages to unnecessary group chats and threads. This type of clutter can be overwhelming and can lead to missed or delayed communication, which can have serious consequences in both personal and professional relationships.

To evaluate the impact of digital communication clutter on your life, ask yourself the following questions:

- How many unread messages do you have across different messaging apps?
- How many unnecessary group chats or threads are you a part of?
- How often do you miss or delay communication as a result of digital clutter?

- How much time do you spend managing digital communication?

By answering these questions, you can gain a better understanding of how digital communication clutter is affecting your life and develop strategies for managing it.

Digital Device Clutter

Digital device clutter can include everything from too many apps and files to outdated software and hardware. This type of clutter can slow down your device and make it difficult to use, leading to frustration and decreased productivity.

To evaluate the impact of digital device clutter on your life, ask yourself the following questions:

- How many apps do you have on your device?

- How much storage space is taken up by unused or unnecessary apps and files?

- How often do you experience slow device performance?

- How often do you have to update or replace hardware or software?

By answering these questions, you can determine how much digital device clutter is affecting your life and develop strategies for managing it.

Therefore, identifying and evaluating the impact of each type of digital clutter on your life can help you develop effective strategies for managing it. By understanding the negative impact of digital clutter on your productivity and mental health, you can take steps to declutter your digital life and create a more organized and streamlined approach to technology use. Some effective strategies for managing digital clutter include setting boundaries and limits on technology use, regularly deleting unnecessary files and apps, and utilizing productivity tools such as calendars and task managers. By taking these steps, you can reduce the negative impact of digital clutter on your life and improve your overall sense of well-being.

CHAPTER 3

CREATING A DIGITAL ORGANIZATION SYSTEM

Developing a folder and file naming convention

Developing a folder and file naming convention is an important step in managing digital clutter. It can help you keep track of your files, find what you need quickly, and reduce the time you spend searching for documents. A good folder and file naming convention should be easy to understand, consistent, and adaptable to changing needs. Here are some steps you can follow to develop a folder and file naming convention that works for you:

Determine what types of files you have: Before you can develop a folder and file naming convention, you need to determine what types of files you have. This can include documents, images, videos, spreadsheets, and more. Categorizing your files into different types can help you determine how to organize them.

Determine what information to include in the file name: Once you have determined what types of files you have, you can determine what information to include in the file name. The file name should be descriptive and provide information about the contents of the file. This can include the date, the author, the subject matter, or any other relevant information.

Determine the order of the information in the file name: After determining what information to include in the file name, you need to decide on the order of the information. This can depend on what is most important to you and how you plan to search for the files. For example, you may choose to include the date first if you often search for files by date.

Develop a consistent folder structure: A consistent folder structure can make it easier to find files and ensure that files are organized in a logical way. You can start by creating main folders for each type of file, such as "Documents," "Images," and "Videos." Within each main folder, you can create subfolders to further organize your files.

Test your folder and file naming convention: Once you have developed a folder and file naming convention, it is important to test it to ensure that it is effective. Try searching for files using your new naming convention and adjust it as needed. You may also want to get feedback from others to see if they find it easy to use.

Here are some tips for developing a folder and file naming convention that works for you:

Keep it simple

The more complex your folder and file naming convention, the harder it will be to maintain. Keep it simple and easy to understand.

Be consistent

Consistency is key when it comes to folder and file naming conventions. Use the same format for all files and folders to ensure that everything is organized in a logical way.

Use abbreviations

Using abbreviations can help you save space in file names and make them easier to read. However, be careful not to use too many abbreviations, as this can make file names confusing.

Include dates

Including dates in file names can make it easier to find files by date. Use the format YYYY-MM-DD to ensure that files are listed in chronological order.

Use keywords

Using keywords in file names can make it easier to search for files. Include relevant keywords that describe the contents of the file.

Developing a folder and file naming convention can help you stay organized and reduce digital clutter. By following these steps and tips, you can create a system that works for you and makes it easy to find the files you need quickly and efficiently.

Using cloud storage and backup solutions

As digital clutter continues to accumulate, it's important to have a system in place for managing and backing up your files. One solution is to use cloud storage and backup services, which allow you to store your files online and access them from anywhere.

Here are some benefits of using cloud storage and backup solutions:

Access files from anywhere: One of the main benefits of using cloud storage is the ability to access your files from anywhere with an internet connection. This is especially useful if you work remotely or travel frequently. With cloud storage, you can easily access your files from your laptop, tablet, or smartphone.

Automatic backup: Cloud backup solutions provide automatic backup, which means your files are backed up automatically without you having to do anything. This ensures that your files are always safe, even if your computer crashes or is lost.

Collaborate with others: Cloud storage solutions also allow you to collaborate with others on files. You can share files with colleagues, friends, or family members and work on them together in real-time. This can improve productivity and make it easier to share files without having to worry about email attachments.

Save space on your computer: Using cloud storage can also help you save space on your computer. Instead of keeping all your files on your hard drive, you can store them online and only download them when you need them.

Enhanced security: Cloud storage solutions often have enhanced security features to protect your files from cyber attacks and data breaches. This includes encryption, multi-factor authentication, and regular security updates.

When using cloud storage and backup solutions, it's important to choose a reputable provider that has strong security measures in place.

Here are some popular cloud storage and backup solutions to consider:

Google Drive: Google Drive is a popular cloud storage solution that provides 15 GB of free storage. It allows you to store, access, and share files from any device. You can also collaborate with others on documents, spreadsheets, and presentations.

Dropbox: Dropbox is another popular cloud storage solution that provides 2 GB of free storage. It allows you to store, share, and access files from any device. You can also collaborate with others on files and set permissions for who can access them.

iCloud: iCloud is Apple's cloud storage solution that provides 5 GB of free storage. It allows you to store, access, and share files across all your Apple devices. You can also backup your iPhone, iPad, or Mac to iCloud.

OneDrive: OneDrive is Microsoft's cloud storage solution that provides 5 GB of free storage. It allows you to store, access, and share files from any device. You can also collaborate with others on files and use Microsoft Office online.

Carbonite: Carbonite is a cloud backup solution that provides automatic backup for your files. It offers different plans for home and business users, with unlimited storage for one computer.

When using cloud storage and backup solutions, it's important to regularly review and manage your files to avoid digital clutter.

Here are some tips for managing files in the cloud:

Delete files you no longer need: Just like with physical clutter, it's important to regularly review and delete files you no longer need. This can help you free up space and keep your files organized.

Create folders and subfolders: Creating folders and subfolders can help you organize your files in a logical way. This can make it easier to find the files you need quickly.

Use descriptive file names: Using descriptive file names can help you quickly identify what the file is and avoid confusion. Make sure the file name is relevant and accurately describes the contents of the file.

Regularly backup your files: Even with cloud backup solutions, it's important to regularly backup your files to ensure that you have a recent copy of your data in case of a system failure or cyber attack. Set up automatic backup schedules or backup your files manually on a regular basis.

Share files with caution: When sharing files with others, make sure to set appropriate permissions and share only with trusted individuals. This can help prevent unauthorized access to your files and protect your data from being compromised.

Use selective sync: Some cloud storage services offer selective sync, which allows you to choose which files and folders are synced to your computer. This can help you save space on your hard drive and avoid cluttering your computer with unnecessary files.

Consider using encryption: For sensitive files, consider using encryption to protect them from unauthorized access. Some cloud storage services offer encryption options, or you can use third-party encryption software.

Using cloud storage and backup solutions can be a helpful tool for managing digital clutter and keeping your files organized and safe. It's important to choose a reputable provider with strong security measures, regularly manage and backup your files, and use best practices for file organization and sharing. With these strategies in place, you can reduce the negative effects of digital clutter and improve your productivity and mental well-being.

Implementing a digital task manager or productivity app

In today's fast-paced digital world, managing tasks and staying productive can be challenging, especially when dealing with digital clutter. One effective solution to help manage digital clutter and improve productivity is implementing a digital task manager or productivity app. These tools can help you stay organized, prioritize tasks, and keep track of progress, ultimately helping you to achieve your goals and reduce stress.

There are many different digital task managers and productivity apps available, each with unique features and benefits.

Here are some key considerations when selecting and implementing a digital task manager or productivity app:

Determine your needs and goals: Before selecting a digital task manager or productivity app, it's important to determine your specific needs and goals. Consider what features are most important to you, such as task lists, reminders, calendar integration, collaboration, and project tracking. Also, think about your preferred platform (e.g., web-based, mobile app, desktop app) and how you plan to use the tool.

Research options: Once you have identified your needs and goals, research different digital task managers and productivity apps that meet your criteria. Some popular options include Todoist, Trello, Asana, and Notion. Read reviews, compare features and pricing, and consider trial periods or free versions to test out the app before committing.

Set up your task manager or productivity app: After selecting an app, set it up to meet your needs. This may involve creating task lists, setting deadlines and reminders, and integrating with your calendar or email.

Take some time to explore all of the features and customize the app to suit your preferences.

Use the app consistently: Consistent use is key to getting the most out of a digital task manager or productivity app. Make a habit of using the app to track tasks, set reminders, and monitor progress. Update your tasks regularly and review your progress regularly to stay on track.

Implementing a digital task manager or productivity app can have many benefits, including improved organization, increased productivity, and reduced stress. By selecting the right tool for your needs, setting it up effectively, and using it consistently, you can manage digital clutter and achieve your goals with greater ease and efficiency.

CHAPTER 4

CLEANING UP YOUR DIGITAL DEVICES

Reducing the number of apps and programs on your devices

In today's digital age, it's easy to accumulate a large number of apps and programs on our devices. While these tools can be useful and entertaining, they can also contribute to digital clutter, reducing productivity and causing stress. One effective solution to manage digital clutter is to reduce the number of apps and programs on your devices. This can help you streamline your digital life and improve your productivity and well-being.

Here are some strategies to help you reduce the number of apps and programs on your devices:

Identify essential apps and programs

Begin by identifying the apps and programs that are essential to your work or personal life. These may include productivity tools, communication apps, and essential software for your job. Make a list of these essential tools to ensure that you do not delete any important apps or programs.

Delete unused apps and programs

Next, review your device and identify apps and programs that you no longer use or need. These may include games, social media apps, or apps that you have downloaded but never used. Delete these apps to free up space on your device and reduce clutter.

Consolidate similar apps

If you have multiple apps that serve similar purposes, consider consolidating them into a single app. For example, if you have multiple email apps, choose one that you prefer and delete the others. This can help you streamline your device and reduce the number of apps you need to manage.

Use web-based tools

Consider using web-based tools instead of installing apps on your device. For example, instead of installing a news app, use a news website. This can help you reduce the number of apps on your device and streamline your digital life.

Evaluate new apps and programs before installing

Before installing a new app or program, evaluate whether it is necessary and will add value to your life. Research the app or program, read reviews, and consider whether it aligns with your needs and goals.

By reducing the number of apps and programs on your devices, you can manage digital clutter, improve productivity, and reduce stress. Identify essential apps, delete unused apps, consolidate similar apps, use web-based tools, and evaluate new apps before installing. With these strategies in place, you can streamline your digital life and achieve greater efficiency and well-being.

Organizing desktop icons and files

The desktop of your computer can be a hot spot for digital clutter. As we accumulate more and more files and documents on our devices, it can become difficult to keep everything organized and easy to find. In this context, organizing desktop icons and files can play a crucial role in managing digital clutter, improving productivity, and reducing stress.

Here are some strategies to help you organize desktop icons and files:

Remove unnecessary icons

Begin by removing unnecessary icons from your desktop. These may include icons for programs that you no longer use, shortcuts to files that you no longer need, or icons for programs that are already in your taskbar or start menu. By reducing the number of icons on your desktop, you can reduce visual clutter and improve your focus.

Use folders

Create folders on your desktop to organize similar files and documents. For example, you may create a folder for work-related documents, a folder for personal documents, or a folder for frequently accessed files. Use clear and descriptive names for your folders to help you find what you need quickly.

Group icons

Group related icons together on your desktop. For example, you may group all your productivity tools in one area and all your entertainment tools in another. This can help you find what you need more easily and reduce the time you spend searching for specific icons.

Use shortcuts

Use shortcuts to access frequently used programs and files quickly. This can help you reduce the number of icons on your desktop while still providing quick access to the tools you need. You can create shortcuts by right-clicking on a program or file and selecting "Create Shortcut."

Keep your desktop clean

Make a habit of regularly cleaning your desktop by deleting files and folders that you no longer need. This can help you maintain a clean and organized desktop, reducing visual clutter and improving your focus.

By organizing desktop icons and files, you can manage digital clutter, improve productivity, and reduce stress. Remove unnecessary icons, use folders, group icons, use shortcuts, and keep your desktop clean. With these strategies in place, you can streamline your digital life and achieve greater efficiency and well-being.

Clearing out old emails, photos, and documents

Emails, photos, and documents can quickly pile up, leading to digital clutter that can hinder productivity and cause stress.

Clearing out old emails, photos, and documents is an important step in managing digital clutter and ensuring that your digital life remains organized and efficient.

Here are some strategies to help you clear out old emails, photos, and documents:

Sort your emails

Start by sorting your emails into categories such as important, spam, and promotional emails. You can also create categories for emails related to work, personal life, and hobbies. Once you have sorted your emails, delete those that are no longer needed, such as promotional emails that are no longer relevant.

Unsubscribe from unnecessary mailing lists

Unsubscribe from mailing lists that you no longer read or are no longer interested in. This can reduce the amount of email clutter in your inbox and ensure that you only receive emails that are relevant to you.

Archive important emails

Archive important emails that you want to keep but don't need to access regularly. This can help reduce clutter in your inbox while ensuring that you have access to important information when you need it.

Delete duplicate photos

Use a photo management tool to delete duplicate photos and those that are blurry or low quality. This can free up space on your device and ensure that you only keep the best photos.

Organize your photos

Organize your photos into folders by date, event, or subject. This can help you find specific photos more easily and reduce visual clutter.

Delete old documents

Delete old documents that are no longer relevant or necessary. This can free up space on your device and make it easier to find the documents that you need.

Backup important files

Before deleting any files, make sure to backup important files to an external hard drive or cloud storage. This can ensure that you don't accidentally delete important files and have a backup in case of a device failure.

By clearing out old emails, photos, and documents, you can manage digital clutter, free up space on your devices, and ensure that your digital life remains organized and efficient. Sort your emails, unsubscribe from unnecessary mailing lists, archive important emails, delete duplicate photos, organize your photos, delete old documents, and backup important files. With these strategies in place, you can maintain an organized and streamlined digital life.

CHAPTER 5

MAINTAINING A CLUTTER-FREE DIGITAL LIFE

Establishing a regular digital decluttering routine

Establishing a regular digital decluttering routine is essential for maintaining an organized and efficient digital life. Just as you might regularly clean out your physical space, such as your closet or pantry, setting aside time to declutter your digital space can help you stay on top of digital clutter and prevent it from getting out of control.

Here are some tips for establishing a regular digital decluttering routine:

Schedule regular decluttering sessions

Set aside time each week or month to declutter your digital space. This could be as simple as spending 30 minutes on a Sunday afternoon to go through your emails or dedicating a few hours on a weekend to organize your digital files.

Start small

Don't try to tackle everything at once. Start with a small area, such as your desktop or email inbox, and work your way through each area of your digital life over time.

Use a checklist

Create a checklist of areas to declutter, such as your email inbox, desktop, photos, and documents. Use this checklist to keep track of what you have done and what still needs to be done.

Delete old and unnecessary files

Delete old and unnecessary files that are taking up space on your device. Be ruthless and ask yourself if you really need each file. If not, delete it.

Unsubscribe from mailing lists

Unsubscribe from mailing lists that you no longer read or are no longer interested in. This can help reduce the amount of email clutter in your inbox and ensure that you only receive emails that are relevant to you.

Use digital organization tools

Use digital organization tools such as file naming conventions, cloud storage, and productivity apps to help keep your digital life organized.

Backup important files

Before deleting any files, make sure to backup important files to an external hard drive or cloud storage. This can ensure that you don't accidentally delete important files and have a backup in case of a device failure.

Evaluate your digital habits

Take a step back and evaluate your digital habits. Are you downloading too many apps or hoarding files? Are you spending too much time on social media? Identifying these habits can help you make changes to prevent digital clutter from accumulating in the future.

Create a system for incoming digital clutter

Just like with physical clutter, it's important to have a system for dealing with incoming digital clutter. For example, you could set up filters in your email inbox to automatically sort incoming messages into different folders, or you could designate a specific folder on your desktop for new files that need to be organized.

Consolidate similar files and folders

If you have multiple files or folders that are similar, consider consolidating them into a single location. This can help reduce clutter and make it easier to find what you need.

Use the 80/20 rule

The 80/20 rule states that 80% of the effects come from 20% of the causes. In the context of digital clutter, this means that you likely only use a small percentage of your files, apps, and programs regularly. Identify the 20% that you use the most and focus on organizing those first.

Set boundaries

Establish boundaries for your digital life to prevent clutter from accumulating in the first place. For example, you could limit the number of apps you download, set a time limit for social media, or unsubscribe from newsletters that aren't adding value to your life.

Don't forget about digital clutter on your phone

While it's important to declutter your computer, don't forget about the digital clutter on your phone. Consider going through your apps and deleting any that you no longer use or need. You can also use similar organization strategies on your phone as you do on your computer, such as creating folders for apps or setting up filters in your email.

Remember, establishing a regular digital decluttering routine is a process. It may take some trial and error to find what works best for you. The important thing is to stay consistent and make digital decluttering a part of your regular routine. With time and effort, you can create a more organized and efficient digital life.

Staying mindful of digital clutter as you work and play

Digital clutter can accumulate quickly and easily, making it important to be mindful of it in our everyday activities. Here are some tips to help you stay mindful of digital clutter as you work and play:

Limit distractions

One of the main sources of digital clutter is distractions. Notifications from apps, email, and social media can pull your attention away from what you're working on and create a sense of overload. To limit distractions, turn off notifications for apps that aren't critical to your work or personal life. Consider setting specific times of the day to check email and social media instead of constantly checking them throughout the day.

Avoid multitasking

Multitasking can also contribute to digital clutter, as it can be tempting to keep multiple tabs or programs open at once. However, this can quickly lead to a cluttered and overwhelming digital workspace. Instead, focus on one task at a time and close out unnecessary tabs and programs to keep your digital workspace organized and focused.

Be mindful of downloads

Downloads, whether they be files or apps, can quickly add to digital clutter. Before downloading anything, ask yourself if you really need it and if it will add value to your digital life. Be mindful of where you're downloading from as well, as some sources may contain malware or other harmful files that can clutter up your digital devices.

Regularly review and delete

It's important to regularly review and delete files, apps, and other digital clutter that you no longer need or use. Schedule time in your calendar to review your digital devices and delete anything that is no longer necessary. This can help prevent digital clutter from building up over time and make it easier to find what you need.

Practice digital minimalism

Digital minimalism is the practice of intentionally limiting the digital tools and technologies you use to only those that are essential to your work and personal life. By practicing digital minimalism, you can reduce the amount of digital clutter in your life and focus on what's truly important.

Use bookmarks

Bookmarks can be a great tool to help you organize your web browsing and keep your digital workspace clutter-free. Instead of keeping multiple tabs open at once, save your favorite websites as bookmarks. This can help you quickly access them without cluttering up your digital workspace.

Use a unified inbox

If you have multiple email accounts, it can be easy to lose track of messages and miss important information. Consider using a unified inbox, which allows you to access all of your emails in one place. This can help you stay organized and reduce the amount of clutter in your email accounts.

Unsubscribe from unnecessary emails

Email newsletters and promotions can quickly fill up your inbox and add to digital clutter. Take the time to unsubscribe from emails that you no longer need or want. This can help you keep your inbox organized and make it easier to find important messages.

Use labels and filters

Labels and filters are powerful tools that can help you organize your digital life. They allow you to sort and categorize emails, files, and other digital content, making it easier to find what you need. Consider setting up labels and filters in your email accounts and other digital tools to keep your digital life organized and efficient.

Don't be afraid to delete

It can be tempting to hold onto digital content, even if you no longer need it. However, holding onto unnecessary files, photos, and other content can quickly lead to digital clutter. Don't be afraid to delete things that you no longer need or use. This can help you keep your digital devices organized and efficient.

Keep your desktop clean

Your desktop is often the first thing you see when you turn on your computer, so it's important to keep it clean and organized. Avoid cluttering your desktop with files, folders, and other digital content. Instead, use folders to organize your files and keep your desktop clean and clutter-free.

Be selective with social media

Social media can be a major source of digital clutter, with constant updates and notifications. Be selective with the social media platforms you use and consider limiting the number of accounts you have. This can help you reduce the amount of digital clutter in your life and create a more intentional online presence.

Staying mindful of digital clutter as you work and play can help you prevent it from accumulating in the first place. By limiting distractions, avoiding multitasking, being mindful of downloads, regularly reviewing and deleting, and practicing digital minimalism, you can create a more organized and efficient digital life.

Enlisting the help of others in your digital decluttering efforts

Decluttering your digital life can be a daunting task, especially if you have accumulated a lot of digital clutter over time. However, you don't have to go it alone. Enlisting the help of others can make the process easier, more fun, and more effective. Here are some ways to get others involved in your digital decluttering efforts:

Enlist the help of a friend or family member

Having someone else to help you declutter can make the process more enjoyable and productive. Ask a friend or family member to help you go through your digital content, such as photos or files, and decide what to keep and what to delete. They can provide a fresh perspective and help you make tough decisions.

Join a digital decluttering group

There are many online communities dedicated to digital decluttering and minimalism. Joining a group can provide you with support, motivation, and accountability as you work to simplify your digital life. You can share your progress, ask for advice, and get inspiration from others who are on the same journey.

Hire a professional organizer

If you're feeling overwhelmed by your digital clutter, consider hiring a professional organizer who specializes in digital decluttering. They can provide expert advice and support, as well as help you create a customized plan for decluttering your digital life. This can be especially helpful if you have a large amount of digital clutter or are struggling to get started.

Take a digital detox challenge with friends

Challenge your friends or family members to a digital detox challenge. Set a goal to limit your screen time or social media use for a certain period of time, such as a week or a month. This can help you break bad digital habits, reduce distractions, and focus on more meaningful activities.

Involve your colleagues

If you work in a team or office, consider getting your colleagues involved in your digital decluttering efforts. You can organize a digital decluttering day or week, where everyone works together to clean up their digital spaces. This can create a more organized and efficient work environment, and improve productivity and collaboration.

Involve your family in creating digital boundaries

It's important to establish digital boundaries within your family to promote healthy habits and reduce digital clutter. Involve your family members in creating these boundaries to ensure everyone is on the same page. You can set limits on screen time, establish tech-free zones in the house, and encourage digital-free activities, such as reading or outdoor activities.

Encourage your children to declutter their digital spaces

Children today grow up surrounded by digital technology and may accumulate a lot of digital clutter. Encourage your children to declutter their digital spaces, such as their smartphones or tablets. Teach them to organize their files and photos, and regularly delete apps or files they no longer use. This can help them develop good digital habits and reduce digital distractions.

Participate in community digital decluttering events

Many communities organize digital decluttering events or e-waste recycling programs. Participating in these events can not only help you declutter your own digital life, but also contribute to a more sustainable and responsible use of digital technology. You can recycle old electronics, donate old devices, or learn more about digital security and privacy.

Use social media mindfully

Social media can be a major source of digital clutter and distraction. Make sure to use social media mindfully by setting boundaries, such as limiting the time you spend on social media or unfollowing accounts that do not bring you joy. You can also organize your social media accounts by using tools such as lists or folders, and regularly declutter your social media feeds by unfollowing accounts that no longer interest you.

Practice self-reflection and evaluation

It's important to regularly reflect on your digital clutter and evaluate your progress. Take time to assess your digital spaces and identify areas that need improvement. Reflect on how your digital clutter affects your productivity, mental health, and overall wellbeing. This can help you stay motivated, focused, and accountable as you continue to simplify your digital life.

Involving others in your digital decluttering efforts can provide valuable support, motivation, and accountability. Whether it's enlisting the help of a friend, joining a digital decluttering group, or involving your family in creating digital boundaries, there are many ways to make the process more enjoyable and effective. By working together, we can create a more intentional and mindful use of digital technology and reduce the negative effects of digital clutter on our productivity and mental health.

CHAPTER 6

THE BENEFITS OF A CLUTTER-FREE DIGITAL LIFE

Improved productivity and focus

One of the most significant benefits of a clutter-free digital life is improved productivity and focus. Digital clutter can be a major source of distraction and overwhelm, making it difficult to stay focused and productive. By decluttering our digital spaces, we can create a more streamlined and efficient workflow that allows us to stay on task and accomplish more.

Here are some ways that a clutter-free digital life can improve our productivity and focus:

Reduced distractions

Digital clutter, such as unnecessary notifications, unread emails, and unused apps, can create constant distractions and interruptions. When we are constantly bombarded with notifications and alerts, it's difficult to stay focused on the task at hand. By decluttering our digital spaces, we can reduce these distractions and create a more peaceful and focused work environment.

Faster access to important information

When our digital spaces are cluttered and disorganized, it can be difficult to find the information we need quickly. By organizing our files, emails, and documents, we can create a more efficient system for accessing the information we need. This can save us time and frustration and allow us to focus more on our work.

More efficient workflow

A clutter-free digital life can also lead to a more efficient workflow. By organizing our digital spaces, we can create a system for prioritizing our tasks and managing our time effectively. This can help us to work more efficiently and accomplish more in less time.

Reduced stress and overwhelm

Digital clutter can contribute to feelings of stress and overwhelm. When we have too many unread emails, unorganized files, and unused apps, it can create a sense of chaos and disorganization in our digital lives. By decluttering our digital spaces, we can reduce these feelings of stress and overwhelm and create a more peaceful and focused work environment.

Improved creativity and inspiration

A clutter-free digital life can also lead to improved creativity and inspiration. When we are not constantly distracted by digital clutter, we can focus more on our creative work and allow our minds to wander and explore new ideas. This can lead to increased inspiration and innovation in our work.

Enhanced collaboration and communication

A clutter-free digital life can also improve collaboration and communication in the workplace. When digital spaces are cluttered and disorganized, it can be difficult to share files and information with colleagues. By establishing a system for organizing files and documents, teams can work more efficiently and effectively together.

Increased security

Digital clutter can also pose a security risk, as sensitive information can become lost or exposed in the clutter. By regularly decluttering and organizing digital spaces, individuals and organizations can ensure that sensitive information is properly secured and protected.

Improved work-life balance

A clutter-free digital life can also lead to improved work-life balance. When we are constantly overwhelmed by digital clutter, it can be difficult to disconnect from work and focus on our personal lives. By decluttering our digital spaces and creating a more efficient workflow, we can reduce the amount of time we spend on work tasks and allow more time for relaxation and personal activities.

Increased confidence and satisfaction

When our digital spaces are cluttered and disorganized, it can contribute to feelings of inadequacy and frustration. By decluttering and organizing our digital spaces, we can feel more confident in our ability to manage our work and personal lives. This can lead to increased satisfaction and a greater sense of accomplishment in our work.

Reduced environmental impact

Finally, a clutter-free digital life can also have a positive impact on the environment. By reducing the number of unnecessary digital files, emails, and apps, we can help to reduce the carbon footprint associated with data storage and processing. This can contribute to a more sustainable and environmentally-friendly digital landscape.

Ultimately, a clutter-free digital life can have a significant impact on our productivity, focus, and overall well-being. By implementing strategies for decluttering and organizing our digital spaces, we can create a more efficient and streamlined workflow, improve collaboration and communication, and reduce stress and overwhelm. Furthermore, a clutter-free digital life can lead to increased security, improved work-life balance, increased confidence and satisfaction, and a reduced environmental impact. By prioritizing digital decluttering, we can create a more peaceful and productive work environment and improve our overall quality of life.

Reduced stress and anxiety

In today's world, where technology has become an integral part of our lives, digital clutter has become a major source of stress and anxiety. A cluttered digital life can lead to a constant feeling of being overwhelmed, which can cause significant stress and anxiety. Fortunately, a clutter-free digital life can help reduce this stress and anxiety.

Here are some ways that a clutter-free digital life can reduce stress and anxiety:

Improved focus and concentration

A clutter-free digital life can help improve focus and concentration. When we have too many files, apps, and notifications vying for our attention, it can be difficult to focus on important tasks. By decluttering our digital spaces, we can reduce distractions and allow ourselves to focus on the task at hand.

Reduced decision fatigue

Digital clutter can also contribute to decision fatigue. When we are constantly bombarded with choices about which file to open or which app to use, it can be mentally exhausting. By reducing the number of choices we have to make, we can conserve mental energy and reduce stress and anxiety.

Increased sense of control

When our digital spaces are cluttered and disorganized, it can contribute to feelings of being out of control. By decluttering and organizing our digital spaces, we can regain a sense of control over our digital lives, which can reduce feelings of stress and anxiety.

Reduced digital overwhelm

Digital overwhelm is a common source of stress and anxiety. When we have too many emails, notifications, and apps vying for our attention, it can be overwhelming. By decluttering our digital spaces and implementing systems to manage our digital lives, we can reduce the feeling of overwhelm and create a more manageable digital landscape.

Improved sleep

Digital clutter can also contribute to poor sleep quality. When we are constantly checking our phones and responding to emails before bed, it can interfere with our ability to fall asleep and stay asleep. By decluttering our digital spaces and establishing boundaries around our digital lives, we can create a more restful environment that promotes better sleep.

Other ways in which digital clutter reduction can reduce stress and anxiety is by improving the overall functioning of our brains. Research suggests that digital clutter and disorganization can lead to a cognitive overload, which means that our brains have to work harder to process information and make decisions. When we have too many notifications, tabs, and open apps, our brains struggle to filter out the unnecessary information and focus on the task at hand. This can lead to mental exhaustion and decreased cognitive function, ultimately impacting our productivity and well-being. By reducing digital clutter, we can help our brains operate more efficiently and effectively. This can lead to increased focus, improved memory, and better decision-making skills. Additionally, a clutter-free digital environment can reduce the distractions that often contribute to stress and anxiety, allowing us to be more present in the moment and better manage our emotions.

A clutter-free digital life can help us develop better habits and routines, which can be key to managing stress and anxiety. By establishing a regular digital decluttering routine and implementing productivity tools, we can create a sense of control over our digital lives and reduce the overwhelming feeling of being constantly "plugged in." This can help us feel more empowered and less anxious about the impact of technology on our lives. Reducing digital clutter can have a significant impact on our mental health and well-being. By taking steps to declutter our digital environments, we can improve our productivity, reduce stress and anxiety, and develop better habits and routines. While the process of decluttering can be challenging, the benefits are well worth the effort.

More time and energy for the things that matter most

A clutter-free digital life can also provide us with more time and energy to focus on the things that matter most in our lives. When we are constantly bombarded by notifications and distracted by digital clutter, it can be difficult to carve out time for the activities and relationships that truly fulfill us. By decluttering our digital lives, we can reduce the time we spend scrolling through social media or searching for lost files, and instead, use that time for activities that bring us joy and fulfillment. This can include spending time with loved ones, pursuing hobbies and interests, or simply taking time for self-care and relaxation.

Furthermore, a clutter-free digital environment can help us establish better work-life balance, which is crucial for maintaining our overall well-being. When we are able to disconnect from our devices and focus on our personal lives outside of work, we are better able to recharge and return to our professional responsibilities with renewed energy and focus. Reducing digital clutter can also help us establish better boundaries in our personal and professional lives. By implementing productivity tools and establishing a regular digital decluttering routine, we can set aside designated times to focus on work and personal responsibilities without the distraction of unnecessary digital clutter.

In addition, a clutter-free digital life can help us feel more in control of our time and energy. By reducing the overwhelm of digital clutter, we can create a sense of calm and clarity that can extend to other areas of our lives. This can help us feel more empowered to make intentional choices about how we spend our time and energy, and ultimately lead to a greater sense of fulfillment and satisfaction.

In conclusion, a clutter-free digital life can provide us with more time and energy to focus on the things that matter most in our lives. By reducing the distractions and overwhelm of digital clutter, we can prioritize the activities and relationships that truly fulfill us, establish better work-life balance, and feel more in control of our time and energy.

Printed in Great Britain
by Amazon

24783521R00073